The
Foundations of
Hip-Hop
Encyclopedia

The Foundations of Hip-Hop Encyclopedia is part of the Virginia Tech Student Publications series. This series contains book-length works authored and edited by Virginia Tech undergraduate and graduate students and published in collaboration with Virginia Tech Publishing. Often these books are the culmination of class projects for advanced or capstone courses. The series provides the opportunity for students to write, edit, and ultimately publish their own books for the world to learn from and enjoy.

The
Foundations
of Hip-Hop
Encyclopedia

*A Class Project by Students in
the Department of Sociology at Virginia Tech*

Edited by
Anthony Kwame Harrison
and
Craig E. Arthur

VIRGINIA TECH
DEPARTMENT OF SOCIOLOGY

VIRGINIA TECH.
PUBLISHING

BLACKSBURG • VIRGINIA

ISBN: 978-1-949373-13-4 (paperback)
ISBN: 978-1-949373-14-1 (PDF)
ISBN: 978-1-949373-15-8 (epub)

DOI: https://doi.org/10.21061/foundations-of-hip-hop

Front cover art by Isabella J. M. Land with design by Lauren Holt.

Back cover art by GoodHomieSigns with design by Lauren Holt.

Acknowledgments

This first edition of *The Foundations of Hip-Hop Encyclo-pedia* was authored by students in the spring 2019 Foundations of Hip-Hop (Topics in Africana Studies/Culture) course taught at Virginia Tech. Participating students in the course each selected an entry topic from a list of over a hundred potential topics. This list was compiled by the editors and included important elements and practices, organizations and record labels, places and artifacts, phenomena and subgenres, and pioneers and personalities. Notably, outside of a handful of key individuals, including important deejays, we chose not to include popular recording artists. Including such artists, we believed, could initiate unresolvable debate over who was and who was not included. In addition, we felt that asking students to write about celebrity personalities could encourage a form of journalistic zeal that, quite frankly, we were hoping to avoid. In the place of recording artists, our list included important albums and songs. We admit that this brings many of the same complications (that is, questions of what gets included and *fan*tastic, or fan-like, writing) as recording artists; however, we also felt that focusing on pieces of music rather than people would help mitigate some of these problems.

Each entry has an approximate word length of either three hundred, five hundred, or seven hundred words. Students were instructed to do independent research into their selected topic. They then met as groups organized around common themes to peer-review and discuss their entry drafts with one another. While maintaining the encyclopedic character of a reference book meant to supply general and, to a certain degree, comprehensive information on a given topic, we also encouraged each contributor to take ownership of the topic and, when warranted, to make an original and personal contribution to the body of knowledge surrounding it. As editors, we are thrilled with the contributions. Acknowledging the limited overall number of entries, we feel that what we have compiled fulfills the terms and expectations of an encyclopedia focusing on foundational aspects of Hip-Hop and its history. At the same time, we feel that each entry conveys something of the distinct character of young people, most of whom were born around the turn of the twenty-first century (long after any of the topics they have written about came into being), reflecting back on the foundations that helped to establish the music and culture that for many continues to entertain, motivate, teach, and inspire. Whereas the number of entries in this first edition is small, we expect that this will be an ongoing project that future iterations of the class can contribute to.

A final note surrounds spelling and other treatments of words. Other than as proper names (for example, DJ Kool Herc), we have chosen to go with the spellings *deejay* and *emcee* for consistency. Following a lively in-class debate, the students decided (via majority vote) to spell Hip-Hop with two capitalized H's and a hyphen: *Hip-Hop*. Also, when an author of an entry uses a word that is also a separate entry in the encyclopedia, that word has been set in **bold** typeface to indicate to the reader there is more in the encyclopedia to read on that subject.

Introduction

The writer James McBride once referred to the founding of Hip-Hop as "the most important cultural event of [his] lifetime" (2007). By this he meant that Hip-Hop, with its irrepressible force and defiant spirit, transformed the global popular music landscape in a way that no music had or has since, arguably, the arrival of swing jazz in the 1930s. Starting from a singular point of origin, or origin story (Harrison 2009), Hip-Hop encapsulates the temporal and spatial framings of the African diaspora. It crystalizes at a distinct postindustrial moment in the history of American labor and race relations (Rose 1994), catalyzed by particular technological innovations. Yet it signals the unfulfilled promises of postbellum society, most immediately "America's short-lived federal commitment" to the supposed achievements of the Civil Rights movement (Rose 1994, 22). At the same time, Hip-Hop fed off of the cultural dynamism of 1970s New York City—an urban landscape that included descendants of enslaved Africans from the US North, the US South, as well as the Anglophone and Hispanophone Caribbean. Furthermore, its emancipatory bravado and political urgency have resonated with black and other marginalized communities wherever its sounds and sentiments have spread.

Most commentators on Hip-Hop recognize it as a constellation of black diasporic practices and priorities, which came together in 1970s New York around a handful of distinct yet interconnected expressive traditions. These "elements," as they are often called, include particular approaches to music composition (deejaying), dancing (breaking), public visual art (graffiti writing), and vocal performance (emceeing). Starting from this four-element model, Hip-Hop aficionados regularly discuss and debate additional elements. For example, music composition practices have ridden the technological wave from deejays' live manipulation of vinyl records to more deliberate practices of Hip-Hop beat-making (Schloss 2014). At various moments claims have been made for beatboxing, fashion, and knowledge (Gosa 2015) as important elements. As an offshoot of this last candidate, we join scholars like Justin Williams (2011) in suggesting that knowledge of Hip-Hop's history and foundations is uniquely important to validating membership in the imagined Hip-Hop nation (Anderson 1983). It is in this spirit that we are delighted to present the first edition of *The Foundations of Hip-Hop Encyclopedia*. The encyclopedia is conceived of as a general reference for students doing work on Hip-Hop's historical dimensions or interested in learning about some of the fundamental practices, principles, and contexts around which this all-important cultural phenomenon developed.

Of all the platforms where Hip-Hop has etched its mark, the arena of education may be the most notable. On the surface Hip-Hop would seem to both defy and embrace education. Many of its heroes were educated in the "school of hard knocks," credentialed through their entanglements with the criminal justice system rather than through conventional schooling. Yet from its very beginnings as a recorded music form, a significant strand of Hip-Hop songs has championed education, if not school itself, as an important means to self-understanding and social understanding. Following a West African tradition of griots, praise poets, and instructive storytellers, Hip-Hop's most ardent social commentators are unquestionable examples of what Italian philosopher Antonio Gramsci (1971) called "organic intellectuals." That Hip-Hop has been so embraced within academic spaces then should come as little surprise. *The Foundations of Hip-Hop Encyclopedia* follows from a more than twenty-year history that includes the establishment of Hip-Hop courses, conferences, and academic journals throughout the United States as well as the world. That the origins of this particular text began in the classroom make it all the more fitting.

As editors of *The Foundations of Hip-Hop Encyclopedia* we wish to thank our student contributors for their enthusiasm, dedication, and professionalism. This volume stands as a testament to the great work that student scholars can produce.

ANTHONY KWAME HARRISON & CRAIG E. ARTHUR
BLACKSBURG, VIRGINIA

References:

Anderson, B. *Imagined Communities*. New York: Verso, 1983.

Gosa, T. L. "The Fifth Element: Knowledge." In *The Cambridge Companion to Hip-Hop*, edited by J. A. Williams, 56–70. Cambridge, UK: Cambridge University Press, 2015.

Gramsci, A. *Selections from the Prison Notebooks*. Edited and translated by Q. Hoare, and G. N. Smith. New York: International Publishers, 1971.

Harrison, A. K. *Hip Hop Underground: The Integrity and Ethics of Racial Identification*. Philadelphia, PA: Temple University Press, 2009.

McBride, J. "Hip Hop Planet." *National Geographic*, 2007. http://ngm.nationalgeographic.com/2007/04/hip-hop-planet/.

Rose, T. *Black Noise: Rap Music and Black Culture in Contemporary America*. Middletown, CT: Wesleyan University Press, 1994.

Schloss, J. G. *Making Beats: The Art of Sample-Based Hip-Hop*. Middletown, CT: Wesleyan University Press, 2014.

Williams, J. "Historicizing the Breakbeat: Hip-Hop's Origins and Authenticity." *Lied und populäre Kultur/Song and Popular Culture* (2011): 133–67.

The

Foundations of Hip-Hop Encyclopedia

A

Afrocentric Political Rap

In its most basic understanding, Afrocentric political rap is a subgenre of Hip-Hop music known as socially conscious rap (awareness of social and political issues surrounding black communities). The purpose of socially conscious rap is to challenge the dominant narratives relating to society, culture, politics, and economics. Through these means, it allows a platform for the voices, stories, and experiences of the black community to be heard. Specifically, black youth used political rap in order to raise consciousness about the historic oppression and injustices experienced by their community. While Afrocentric political rap is most certainly an important subgenre of Hip-Hop, knowing its development is equally as important.

The early development of Afrocentric political rap begins with the emergence of the golden age of Hip-Hop, which many would agree dates back to the 1980s and early 1990s. It is important to note that before the eighties and nineties, the Black Power movement, led by the Black Panther Party, played a pivotal role in inspiring the emergence of Afrocentric political rap. All throughout the eighties and early nineties, artists like Public Enemy, Sister Souljah, the Jungle Brothers, and X-Clan all possessed aspects of socially and politically conscious Afrocentricity. These artists, through their politically and socially aware music, helped to solidify the popularity of Afrocentric political rap as both a memorable and influential subgenre of Hip-Hop.

Additionally, connecting the social and political context to Hip-Hop music helped to unify the voices and experiences of black youth within their communities through personal narratives and storytelling. The specific topics socially conscious rap addresses include but are not limited to institutional racism, incarceration, poverty, violence, police brutality, the criminalization of black people, and drugs.

While socially conscious rap brought about social awareness of the realities of black communities, it also allowed rappers and their crews to advocate for black liberation and solidarity. In relation to social and political contexts, it helped not only to bring awareness but also to assimilate these experiences into a society that slowly, but surely, began to shift its culture towards a more multicultural perspective. The main accomplishment of Afrocentric political rap was to raise social and political consciousness about black experiences, which contributed towards a general understanding of the social, political, and economic context of black communities altogether. Because of the profound influence of Afrocentric political rap in the dominant mainstream, the sociocultural landscape of the communities it hailed from shaped the development of Hip-Hop.

As Afrocentric political rap quickly grew into a highly popular and influential subgenre of Hip-Hop, it became implicated in the shift from socially conscious rap to gangsta rap (a subgenre of Hip-Hop characterized by aggressive tones of violence experienced by black people). Some notable artists within gangsta rap include N.W.A, Ice-T, Tupac, 50 Cent, and Ice Cube. In terms of stylistic elements, gangsta rap is arguably the counterpart to socially conscious rap. Gangsta rap, as compared to Afrocentric political rap, favors more of an aggressive tone and style that exposes the violence, substance abuse, and harsh realities of black communities. The shift from Afrocentric political rap to gangsta rap reflects the complexities of the effects the sociocultural landscape had on the development of Hip-Hop at the time. This narrative and cultural shift from socially conscious rap to gangsta rap represents the constant dynamic of the ever-changing subgenres of Hip-Hop throughout its history.

Understanding the historical development of Afrocentric political rap is necessary to comprehend its current significance. Noteworthy and talented artists like Azealia Banks, Brockhampton, Childish Gambino, Kendrick Lamar, Noname, and Vince Staples are all credited with being socially conscious. For instance, Childish Gambino's "This Is America" is filled with numerous symbols representing the racism and violence experienced by black people. With his racially and politically charged lyrics, Childish Gambino made it clear that racism, oppression, and violence against black communities are far from over. As long as Afrocentric political rap continues to effectively influence Hip-Hop, socially conscious rap will continue to remain prevalent in the politics and culture of our society.

LIAN JOSEPH
VIRGINIA TECH

See also:
AmeriKKKa's Most Wanted, It Takes a Nation of Millions to Hold Us Back, "The Message," "Self Destruction," Straight Outta Compton

Further reading:
Jam, B. "The Rise and Fall of Afrocentric Rap as the Predominant Movement within Hip-Hop." Amoeblog, February 4, 2011. https://www.amoeba. com/blog/2011/02/jamoeblog/the-rise-and-fall-of-afrocentric-rap-as-the-predominant-movement-within-hip-hop.html.

AmeriKKKa's Most Wanted

AmeriKKKa's Most Wanted is the debut studio album by Los Angeles rapper Ice Cube, released on May 16, 1990. The album was produced by the Bomb Squad (the production team for the prominent New York City Afrocentric rap group Public Enemy) and Ice Cube's crew (rap group or friends), Da Lench Mob. Ice Cube was previously known as a member of N.W.A, a revolutionary rap group whose hard beats and explicit lyrics hit America with force and quickly gained popularity and stirred up controversy, revolutionizing gangsta rap. Gangsta rap is a form of Hip-Hop that became the dominant style in the 1990s and was a product of the violent lifestyle of American inner cities rife with discrimination, poverty, and crime. Ice Cube split from N.W.A when he felt he was not being fairly compensated for his contributions to the group.

AmeriKKKa's Most Wanted was praised as a beautiful mix of East Coast and West Coast style rap, which led to its immense success. The album was well received by the public and went certified gold in three months and platinum a year later. However, the album also had its fair share of controversy. Ice Cube's album title can be interpreted two ways. First, by replacing the c in America with KKK, Ice Cube asserted that racism and discrimination were very much still present in 1990s America. Additionally, the "Most Wanted" implies that the racist elite and people in charge will take issue with Ice Cube shedding light on issues such as these. The second meaning of the album title is that Ice Cube is America's most wanted gangster.

The songs and skits on the album blend together seamlessly, with no stops in between, which couples perfectly with Cube's prolific lyrics. In the title song "AmeriKKKa's Most Wanted," Ice Cube spins an enchanting tale explaining the reasons why he is America's most wanted and detailing how he is the best in the game (in the world) at committing crimes. The song draws to a conclusion with Cube robbing a white neighborhood and then subsequently getting arrested after the crime. The most powerful part of the song is when Cube says, "The police didn't pay it no mind" when "I was robbin' my own kind." This highlights how America does not care about black-on-black crime but immediately takes action once a white person is the victim, showing the disproportionality in the criminal justice system. This kind of storytelling is prevalent throughout the whole album. In songs such as "Endangered Species," "Once Upon a Time in the Projects," and "A Gangsta's Fairytale," Cube comments on various injustices black people face in America, such as poverty and police brutality.

AmeriKKKa's Most Wanted was a groundbreaking album that helped usher rap into a new territory of social justice and that told the tales of black Americans' frustrations and angers. The album has influenced many rappers since its release and was even said to influence Biggie Smalls's *Ready to Die*. The concepts discussed in the title song are still prevalent in America today, making it just as relevant as it was upon release.

W. Clyde Bryson IV
Virginia Tech

See also:
Afrocentric Political Rap, *It Takes a Nation of Millions to Hold Us Back*, *Straight Outta Compton*

Further reading:
Coleman, B. "The Making of Ice Cube's 'AmeriKKKa's Most Wanted.'" Cuepoint, October 13, 2014. https://medium.com/cuepoint/ice-cube-check-the-technique-202d2a794008.
Encyclopedia Britannica Online. "Gangsta Rap." By Greg Tate. Last modified November 26, 2013. https://www.britannica.com/art/gangsta-rap.
Martinez, G. "Ice Cube's *AmeriKKKa's Most Wanted* Was a Pivotal Cry for Social Justice." Treble: Music for the Bleeding Edge, May 2, 2017. https://www.treblezine.com/35017-ice-cube-amerikkkas-most-wanted-social-justice/.

B

Beatboxing

Beatboxing is a form of vocal percussion where an artist uses their lips, tongue, and voice to imitate the sounds that are usually produced on a turntable or percussion instrument. Beatboxing is a mainstream cultural aspect of Hip-Hop and was once practiced by many artists. Originating in the 1980s, beatboxing was influenced by many foreign traditions and practices of vocal percussion. Many African musical performers use their bodies and mouths to expel breath in a technique similar to that used today. Although the term *beatboxing* is used broadly, it is often limited to a certain style of vocal percussion connected with Hip-Hop and commonly used within specific urban music genres. Beatboxing is incorporated in popular songs by famous rappers, but it also lives in the streets, where everyday people practice Hip-Hop regularly. Its reach spans from the oldest of Hip-Hop fans to the youngest, all of whom are capable of producing beatbox sounds. The artist Doug E. Fresh is known specifically for his talent in beatboxing. The quick and funky beats made from Fresh's mouth are featured on many classic Hip-Hop tracks. Fresh and the legendary emcee Slick Rick collaborated on several songs, including "The Show" and **"La Di Da Di."**

Phil Patterson
Virginia Tech Football

See also:
Cyphers, "La Di Da Di"

Further reading:
Griffin, D. "History of Beatboxing." Our Pastimes, last modified September 15, 2017. https://ourpastimes.com/history-of-beatboxing-12311301.html.

C

Christmas Rap

Christmas rap is a subgenre of Hip-Hop that focuses on original Christmas-themed content from Hip-Hop artists. Christmas rap has been around since Kurtis Blow utilized the Christmas theme as a way into the top charts with his single "Christmas Rappin'" in late 1979. Christmastime in the New York borough of Harlem has now been registered as a novelty of sorts through Christmas rap.

Opportunity, money, and clout are the most prevalent reasons for Hip-Hop artists to create original Christmas-themed music. Genres that don't provide Christmas-themed content drop in streams and sales during the month leading up to the holidays. This opens an opportunity to supply the demand. Hip-Hop artists transform their general themes into Christmas content in songs like Run-DMC's "Christmas in Hollis," which features classic Hip-Hop themes like chillin' on the ave (hanging out on the avenue) and getting money.

A huge percentage of music revenue in the month between Thanksgiving and Christmas goes to Christmas-themed music. By creating Christmas music for this month, as well as regular content in the other months, Hip-Hop artists guarantee themselves revenue and streams for all months of the year, whereas other artists lose this chance by not creating such music. Hip-Hop artists are more likely to take advantage of this opportunity to make money because most Hip-Hop artists value money as part of the American dream of "making it" after living in struggle for so long.

Hip-Hop artists not only value the money that can be made during Christmas time, they also value the perennial clout that comes from creating seasonal music. If an artist creates a piece that is deemed "quality," it will resurface year after year during the holidays, as Kanye West's "Christmas in Harlem" does every year. There is almost no other way to guarantee such a long-continuing shelf life for a song or album, which creates an opportunity to earn clout.

EMILY GURGANUS
VIRGINIA TECH

The Chronic

Released over a quarter century ago, Dr. Dre's debut solo album, *The Chronic*, portrayed more than simply a glimpse of California's early 1990s Hip-Hop scene. On its release in late 1992, *The Chronic* laid the foundation for the beginning of Death Row Records' transformation of the Hip-Hop industry. In the wake of the 1992 Los Angeles riots—in which South-Central Los Angeles erupted into turmoil due to a trial jury acquitting four Los Angeles police officers for the accused assault and use of excessive force on Rodney King—*The Chronic*'s musical elements mirrored the sights and sounds of the surrounding turmoil. The vivid description of a scraping reality in tracks such as "Lil' Ghetto Boy" illuminated Hip-Hop's viability as a platform to address the pressing issues facing urban communities throughout America. Yet its lively composition combined the talents of young artists from Long Beach and Compton—local youth like Snoop Doggy Dogg, Daz Dillinger, Kurupt, Lady of Rage, RBX, Nate Dogg, and Warren G—who used The Chronic's long-lasting success to establish and maintain solo careers of their own.

Backed by its upbeat melodic singles—"Let Me Ride," "Nuthin' But a 'G' Thang," and "Dre Day"—*The Chronic* brought the particularly regional G-Funk sound to America's pop-culture market. In its production, *The Chronic* linked these nuanced practices of Hip-Hop with the historic characteristics of New York's early 1980s Hip-Hop scene, in which the artistic concept of Hip-Hop was used to describe ongoing social inequities. Moreover, inspired heavily by George Clinton's Parliament Funkadelic, *The Chronic* conjoined melodic synths with heavily distorted drums that intermingled under the sounds of a crisp sample. Backed by an ensemble of unknown young artists, *The Chronic* detailed the perspectives, beliefs, and ideas of the African American youth living in Southern California's inner-city social conditions.

The Chronic's effect on the Hip-Hop industry reached far beyond its musical elements. In its development, *The Chronic* largely employed artists from Death Row Records. These artists, mostly in their late teens and early twenties, developed careers that had a significant impact on the Californian Hip-Hop scene. *The Chronic's* inclusion of Dr. Dre's formidable protégé, Snoop Doggy Dogg, prompted the success of his debut album, **Doggystyle**.

In conclusion, *The Chronic* is nostalgically viewed as a foundational element of Hip-Hop's development on the West Coast. Its vivid descriptions of life in South-Central Los Angeles during the tumultuous early 1990s provide the contemporary Hip-Hop audience with a glimpse of its history as an art form that described the real-life attitudes of Southern Californian youth.

Brett Kershaw
McComas, Virginia Tech

See also:
Afrocentric Political Rap, *Doggystyle*, Sampling

College Radio

During the 1980s Hip-Hop was beginning to gain popularity among the general public, who could hear rap songs being played in clubs or on the streets; however, these songs were still rarely played on radio stations outside of a few major cities across the country. One exception to this was college radio. Therefore, college radio had a strong influence on the acceptance and appreciation of Hip-Hop as a genre in music. College radio influenced the rise in Hip-Hop popularity among young people through much more than just playing Hip-Hop music over the air. College radio allowed African American college students to continue their cultural practices in predominately white institutional environments. Through college radio, students took ideas and community-based values, which they learned from their families and neighborhoods back home, shared them, and created their own distinct groups within university settings.

One purpose of college radio was to inform students of events happening on and off campus, such as rush events, seminars, or live music performances. Another aspect of college radio that was used to engage students and create community was the practice of giving "shout-outs" to friends, sports teams, sororities or fraternities, clubs, or anyone else student radio programmers felt needed a little extra boost of confidence in their day. College radio also allowed African American students to use their interests and passion in an academic manner; for example, students used marketing research methods to figure out what popular up-and-coming artists and songs to play for listeners. People also wanted to hear background information about songs or artists, which required research as well. By engaging in these academic practices and applying them to their passion, many African American students flourished in universities and continued to apply these skills to their careers.

AUDREY COLLIER
VIRGINIA TECH SOCIOLOGY

Further reading:
Harrison, A. K. "Black College-Radio on Predominantly White Campuses: A 'Hip-Hop Era' Student-Authored Inclusion Initiative." *Journal of Pan African Studies* 9, no. 8 (2016): 135–54.

Crossover Rap Hits

Stepping outside of the rap game (the world of rap music) was essential for the internal success of Hip-Hop music. Crossovers were the fuel that rap music needed to break through the stratosphere and into mainstream American pop culture. Oftentimes within cultural discussions, people will mention how diversity of thought is essential for growth and advancement. Diversity is impactful not just because more ideas are a good thing, but because the intersection of differing ideas can be a powerful union, such as in the case of crossover rap hits.

Crossover songs should not be confused with samples or covers. A sample is using part of another preexisting musical work from within Hip-Hop and then applying it to compose part of a new Hip-Hop song. For example, Rob Base and DJ E-Z Rock's 1988 hit "It Takes Two" sampled a vocal riff from Lyn Collins's 1972 song "Think (About It)"—notably the duo did not use the entirety of Collins's song (see **Sampling**). A cover is a music artist's complete rendition of another artist's song. Covers can be susceptible to copyright infringement if the original author does not give written, explicit permission. Covered versions of the original work are typically performed within the same genre as the original. A covered song that crosses over from the original genre into a new genre could be considered a "crossover cover." A crossover song is a song or musical work that appeals to audiences of multiple genres. A good way to define this is if a given song can be ranked on multiple music charts of different genres.

A crossover rap song is a musical work where the **flow** (or smoothness) and rhythmic layering of a rapper's lyrics are overlaid with the rhythmic patterns of other genres, possibly also accompanied by the rigid sounds of Hip-Hop beats. Crossover rap hits have significantly helped perpetuate Hip-Hop's popularity and propelled many rappers and Hip-Hop artists into the mainstream of American music.

Rap began with crossover hits. **"Rapper's Delight"** by the Sugar Hill Gang, released in 1979, is widely regarded as the first official rap song in America. However, it is important to note that this was not the first Hip-Hop song. "Rapper's Delight" is not a Hip-Hop song in that it does not have any elements of Hip-Hop in it—elements which go far beyond the verbal act of rapping lyrics. "Rapper's Delight" is actually a disco-rap crossover. The rhythmic beat and body of the song has a classic 1970s disco-pop tone with rapped lyrics over it. This is what a lot of early rap existed as—rapping over other pop beats because deejays of the time would mix over records in clubs where emcees would rap over those ongoing beats.

It is difficult to overstate the importance of these deejay-led crossover sessions because they ultimately led to the development of Hip-Hop. Crossover rap music created the elements necessary for the Hip-Hop genre to exist, including deejays who mixed records and messed around with beats, and emcees who became increasingly creative with their rapping techniques. This led to the creation of many new sounds, new techniques, and ultimately the birth of Hip-Hop as recorded music through artists like Run-DMC, the Beastie Boys, and LL Cool J, among others.

Perhaps the most famous mainstream crossover rap hit is "Walk This Way (ft. Aerosmith)" by Run-DMC, released in 1986. This crossover helped break the glass ceiling for Hip-Hop artists like Run-DMC, who were widely popular but not yet accepted in mainstream American music. This rap-rock crossover also helped Run-DMC cross over to reach a newer audience, in that many white Americans came to accept the group after their work with the popular rock band Aerosmith. Arguably, the single helped Aerosmith more than Run-DMC, as the band was on a decline in popularity due to drug use and disunity amongst members. Nevertheless, Run-DMC's crossover hit single with Aerosmith played a large role in the beginning of Hip-Hop's acceptance amongst white American audiences and American mainstream pop culture.

Justin McCloskey
Virginia Tech

See also:
Def Jam Records, "Rapper's Delight," Rick Rubin, Sampling, Sugar Hill Records

Further reading:
Young, R. "How 'Walk This Way' Opened Up the Airwaves for Rap and Hip-Hop." *Here & Now*, February 21, 2019. https://www.wbur.org/hereandnow/2019/02/21/walk-this-way-run-dmc-aerosmith.

Cyphers

A cypher is a freestyle rap session involving a group of people. The cypher environment usually consists of two or more emcees who are rapping. To begin, there has to be a meeting place for the rappers. There does not have to be a common topic. In the cypher, emcees create their own vibe (atmosphere) regardless of whether there is instrumental music playing. If there is not an instrumental beat, a clever rapper will organize their lyrics in a way to avoid being distracted. Rappers tend to focus better when there is a consistent tempo and rhythm. Sometimes, in the absence of an instrumental beat, a cypher participant will **beatbox** (a Hip-Hop form of vocal percussion). In a freestyle cypher, rap lyrics are improvised. The randomness of words and topics are of primary importance. A Hip-Hop cypher can essentially be thought of as a lyrical jam session. The cypher builds energy as each emcee improvises spontaneously and the rest of the group feeds off of it. There is an expectation that the rhymes used in a cypher are not previously written. In other words, the rhymes should come straight off the dome (from the rapper's immediate thoughts).

As explained above, the term *cypher* in Hip-Hop is shorthand for "freestyle rap cypher." The meaning behind this is that the lyrics should not be about a particular subject. Similarly, the lyrics should not be memorized beforehand. Prior to cypher becoming a Hip-Hop term, the *Oxford English Dictionary* defined it as a person who fills a place, but is of no importance or worth.

Cyphers have always provided a space for freestyle rapping in Hip-Hop. Before the 1980s, early freestyles included written and memorized raps. The emergence of the improvised freestyle cypher has been credited to a golden era Hip-Hop (late 1980s and early 1990s) emcee named Myka 9. Myka 9, whose given name is Michael Troy, claims that he helped popularize the practice of spontaneously rapping in cyphers. Yet the idea of cyphering in general was established in the Hip-Hop community well before Myka 9's emergence.

TRINITY BAPTISTE
VIRGINIA TECH

See also:
Beatboxing

D

Def Jam Records

Def Jam Records is one of the most successful black-owned record labels in the United States. Def Jam Records was created by **Rick Rubin** and Russel Simmons in New York City in 1984. Rubin and Simmons created an empire. Def Jam Records has an important role in Hip-Hop owing to the fact that the label introduced numerous artists who broke records on the charts and helped build Hip-Hop into what it is today. The Beastie Boys were one of the most well-known groups that first signed to Def Jam Records. Their album *Licensed to III*, released in 1986, climbed to the top of the Billboard charts. This was the first Hip-Hop album to reach the number one spot on the Billboard charts. LL Cool J is another artist that signed early to the Def Jam label and, with his single "I Need a Beat," became one of the first rappers to achieve mainstream success. This helped to create a strong reputation for Def Jam Records. However, Def Jam did not want to be boxed in to only the genre of Hip-Hop. The record label also signed Slayer, a metal band. Def Jam Records increased its appeal to young listeners by incorporating heavy metal and rock into rap music.

Def Jam was innovative in other ways. During the Cash Money Records reign (roughly 1998 to 2012), luxury was a main theme in rap, but during the Def Jam era recording artists introduced storytelling as a key element of Hip-Hop. Def Jam Records also introduced the first major sneaker deal in Hip-Hop. The group Run-DMC became the first Hip-Hop act to receive a million-dollar endorsement deal from Adidas. This opened doors for Hip-Hop artists today, many of whom have endorsement deals. In later years, Def Jam was among the first labels to give record deals to members of already successful rap groups. This opened doors for many Hip-Hop artists.

In 1994, following a series of financial woes, Def Jam partnered with the Dutch music company PolyGram. Then in 1998, after Polygram was purchased by the Universal Music Group, the parent company merged Island Records, Mercury Records, and Def Jam Records to create the Island Def Jam Music Group. Def Jam Germany was launched in 2000, allowing the label to expand internationally. As Def Jam expanded, it came to engulf several smaller record labels, including ARTium Recordings, Desert Storm Records, Disturbing tha Peace, GOOD Music, Radio Killa Records, and Roc-A-Fella Records. These sub-labels are responsible for the emergence of major artists such as Jay-Z and Kanye West. Def Jam Records is a label that recognizes young talent. They recognized Kendrick Lamar at the age of seventeen. In the early 2000s many popular artists released music through Def Jam, including Ludacris, Frank Ocean, Ashanti, Kanye West, Jay-Z, DMX, Rhianna, and Ja Rule. Many of these artists were from different labels that branched off of Def Jam Records. In 2001 Jay-Z's album *The Blueprint* sold over 2.7 million records. The same year, DMX sold over three million copies of his album *The Great Depression.* In 2007 Rhianna hit the big time with her smash album *Good Girl Gone Bad.* The album produced seven singles, including the Grammy-winning song "Umbrella." The album sold close to ten million copies worldwide. Today's Def Jam roster includes Justin Bieber, Alessia Cara, Logic, Pusha T, Jadakiss, Vince Staples, Jeremih, Big Sean, YG, 2 Chainz, Dave East, and Jhené Aiko, among others. Today, led by chairman and CEO Paul Rosenberg, Def Jam has reaffirmed its passion for and commitment to Hip-Hop culture and has expanded its global brand reach to become the most-followed major label on all major social media platforms.

Def Jam has opened plenty of doors, making it foundational to the growth of Hip-Hop. The label helped introduce new video concepts and **sampling** techniques, among other things, that the Hip-Hop community still uses today. Def Jam has had the greatest number of charting songs and charting artists in Hip-Hop, the most cumulative weeks on the charts, and the greatest number of years charting. Although the 2000s may be characterized as the reign of Cash Money Records, if it weren't for Def Jam Records, Hip-Hop would not be the same.

PRESTON HORNE
VIRGINIA TECH

See also:
Crossover Rap Hits, Rick Rubin

Doggystyle

Doggystyle is the debut studio album from rapper Snoop Dogg (then known as Snoop Doggy Dog), released through Death Row Records in 1993. The album introduced a component of Hip-Hop that elevated West Coast culture and helped establish the power of the G-Funk trend. Through Dr. Dre's production, the album featured samples from funk icons such as Isaac Hayes, George Clinton, and Curtis Mayfield. This was a powerful component in the evolution of Hip-Hop.

The songs discuss relevant situations and circumstances from the early 1990s that still resonate today. Snoop Dogg's lyrics utilize great wordplay and vivid imagery as he details the circumstances of living in the inner city of Long Beach, California. The album has notable Hip-Hop classics that are still celebrated over twenty-five years after it was released. "Gin and Juice" showcases Snoop Dogg's calm and laid-back personality and rhyme style, though the song's lyrics describe things such as parties, marijuana, sexual innuendos, and the alcoholic combination that the song is named for. The song has been credited with having one of the most infectious hooks in the history of Hip-Hop. Another notable song is "Lodi Dodi," where Snoop Dogg covers the famous song **"La Di Da Di"** by Doug E. Fresh and featuring Slick Rick. The beat used in the remake is irresistible and has been equated with other heavy-hitting rap songs of the times. "For All My Niggaz & Bitches" (featuring Tha Dogg Pound) is a song with strong wordplay and hard-hitting features taking center stage. In the song, Dogg Pound members Kurupt and Daz arguably outshine Snoop Dogg. This facilitated their budding reputation throughout the Hip-Hop world, which was well deserved since the Dogg Pound played such a key role in the creation of *Doggystyle*.

Through his collaborations with Dr. Dre and the Dogg Pound, Snoop Dogg's debut album is considered ground-breaking. By using samples from funk music of the past, Snoop Dogg, along with his frequent collaborator, Warren G, helped establish the new trend of G-Funk, which is still relevant and continues to inspire Hip-Hop artists today. Beyond creating an ensemble of powerful songs that work together, *Doggystyle* connected the culture of Long Beach with the wider audience for Hip-Hop music. The power of this debut album demonstrated the impact of the gangsta lifestyle and soulful funk that gangsta rap hailing from Long Beach could provide. This is powerful, and this album is Hip-Hop, both synonymous and breathtaking.

Eyoel Fassil
Virginia Tech

See also:
The Chronic, "La Di Da Di," Sampling

E

Enter the Wu-Tang (36 Chambers)

"Cash rules everything around me / CREAM, get the money / Dollar dollar bill, y'all." This is the hook to one of the most recognizable rap songs of all time, "C.R.E.A.M.," the eighth track of the Wu-Tang Clan's debut album, *Enter the Wu-Tang (36 Chambers)*. *Enter the Wu-Tang (36 Chambers)* was released on November 9, 1993, one of the biggest years for rap music. It is one of the most influential albums in the history of Hip-Hop. It facilitated the East Coast Hip-Hop movement's resurgence by foregrounding the hardcore, gritty sound and content that contradicted the West Coast's G-Funk aesthetic. *Enter the Wu-Tang* peaked at number forty-one on the Billboard 200, was certified platinum, and ranks number eight on the list of top R & B/ Hip-Hop albums of 1993. The three singles that came out of the project were "Method Man," "C.R.E.A.M.," and "Can It Be All So Simple." The Wu-Tang Clan consisted of nine members at the time of the album's release: RZA, GZA, Raekwon the Chef, Method Man, Ghostface Killah, Ol' Dirty Bastard, Inspectah Deck, Masta Killa, and U-God. Most of the album was solely produced by RZA.

The martial arts theme that laid the foundation for the album was influenced by the karate movies the members watched. The album begins with dialogue from the movie Shaolin vs. Wu-Tang, which transitions into the intro track, "Bring Da Ruckus." The aggressive lyrics, grimy content, and martial arts sound effects (like sword slashing) that the Wu-Tang Clan brought to this album were collectively called "sword style." Every member of the clan was extremely "sharp" lyrically. Accordingly, they compared their words to swords slicing through their opponents. The production was equally "sharp." The sounds of the beats pierce through listeners' ears and leave a permanent impression on anyone who decides to experience "the way of the Wu."

Arguably, there is something for every Hip-Hop listener on the album's thirteen-song track list. Songs range from the mellowness of "Can It Be All So Simple," to the more serious tone of "Tearz." "C.R.E.A.M." supplies a kick of motivation, whereas battle rap or **cypher** style bars (an alternate term for lyrics) dominate "Protect Ya Neck," "Wu-

Tang: 7th Chamber," and one of the two solo tracks on the album, GZA's "Clan in da Front." Some fans that have carefully studied the album say the members of the clan were sharpest on "Da Mystery of Chessboxin'," the album's sixth track. The song had verses from U-God, Inspectah Deck, Raekwon, Ol' Dirty Bastard, Ghostface Killah, and Masta Killa, who only had one verse on the album, but many say he delivered the best verse in the song. The Wu-Tang Clan pioneered a new sound and style of rap music with *Enter the Wu-Tang (36 Chambers)*. They inspired future rap acts to develop an edgy, hardcore style. This album should be discussed with the highest level of respect, and it is a must listen to.

MICHAEL DUPUY JR. (A.K.A. PEENUT)
STUDENTS OF HIP-HOP LEGACY (SOHHL)
SCHOOL OF VISUAL ARTS
VIRGINIA TECH

See also:
Cyphers, *Doggystyle*

F

Flow

Flow may be defined as rhymes or rhythms that imply fluid, harmonious motion and smoothness without friction or stress. Flow is important to Hip-Hop because flow is the manner, and style, in which an artist delivers his or her message. Flow consists of rhymes and rhythms. These rhymes are important in three different aspects: sentence structure, the rhymes themselves, and their use. Sentence structure refers to the length of the sentence in which the rhymes are used, where they fall in relation to the music, and the density of rhymes used. The importance of the rhymes themselves includes the number of syllables they consist of, where in the sentence the rhymes are used, and if that pattern of placement is repeated or not. The use of the rhymes refers to whether the rhymes themselves are repeated and if new ones are made throughout the song or not.

These aspects are important because they influence flow. Emcees are known, become famous, and listened to, in part, due to their flow. The differentiation between the above characteristics or aspects of rhymes produces different flows. Flow is important to Hip-Hop because it gives a sense of individuality and ownership and in some ways reflects who a rapper or emcee is as an artist. What is most important for artists is not what they say, but how they say it. The way in which they deliver their message is what helps them gain popularity and, if good or unique enough, eventually money.

The concept of flow is not limited to rhymes alone. Hip-Hop was also created and popularized by deejays, breakers (dancers), and graffiti writers with different, unique, and individualized styles of flow. As part of his work in describing the foundations of Hip-Hop, Joseph C. Ewoodzie Jr., in *Break Beats in the Bronx*, lists the three founding fathers of Hip-Hop as Afrika Bambaataa, DJ Kool Herc, and Grandmaster Flash. Each of these deejays and artists had a different flow to the way they would mix music, which brought mass attention to their craft and thus created the foundation for Hip-Hop to gain popularity.

Rhyming flows from the beginning consisted of only a few syllables per bar (musical measure). Since the founding of Hip-Hop, flow has evolved. Since the earliest days of rhyming, new flows have been the primary mechanisms for introducing new waves of rapping styles. A good example of flow transition in Hip-Hop is the recent shift from lyrical rap to mumble rap.

JOHN OSORIO
VIRGINIA TECH

Further reading:

Ewoodzie, J. C. Break Beats in the Bronx: Rediscovering Hip-Hop's Early Years. Chapel Hill: University of North Carolina Press, 2017.

Conner, M. "The Rapper's Flow Encyclopedia." Genius, accessed April 28, 2019. https://genius.com/posts/1669-The-rapper-s-flow-encyclopedia.

G

Gold Chains

Gold chains are the epitome of Hip-Hop in the African American community. While the elements that make up Hip-Hop are deejaying, emceeing, breaking (break dancing), and graffiti, gold chains have been among the most eye-catching Hip-Hop artifacts for decades. The bling (spectacular jewelry) has changed throughout the years from "Jesus pieces" to pinky rings and now diamond-encrusted everything. Jewelry has demonstrated a sense of power and status within the African American community. Hip-Hop has showcased jewelry for nearly fifty years. On his debut album cover, Kurtis Blow became the first rapper to ever appear wearing gold chains. He wore five small chains.

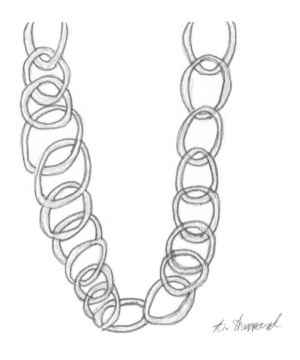

As time continued, rappers and other Hip-Hop artists began to compete with each other to see who had the biggest, flashiest gold chains. In the early nineties, the flex (showing off or gloating) really took a turn when artists began to create diamond pendants that sported (championed) the labels they were loyal to. The 2000s was an era oriented around the principle "bigger is better." This meant that every rapper was judged by the size of their pendant and the length of their chain. The bigger the chain, the more money one was presumed to have. T-Pain began this movement by taking a photo of his $400,000 chain that read "Big A** Chain" and posting it online. He later took the diamonds out of the chain and melted it down to create other smaller chains.

As Hip-Hop continues to grow in all dimensions, it will be fascinating to see how jewelry continues to shape the world of Hip-Hop artistry. Artists today do not need to verbalize their power; they allow their jewelry to do the talking. These pieces of jewelry provide artists with a sense of status among their peers. This means wealth, prestige, and the success that goes along with it. Hip-Hop and gold have always gone hand in hand, and fans look forward to seeing what phenomena will arise to touch their hearts and enhance the sense of unity throughout the Hip-Hop community.

AISHA SHEPPARD
VIRGINIA TECH WOMEN'S BASKETBALL

See also:
Hip-Hop Fashion

H

Hip-Hop Clubs

Hip-Hop clubs were very popular in New York during the 1980s. Clubs were so popular at this time because they were places where the Hip-Hop community could social-ize and meet one another. It is a lot different now because people have technologies that allow them to hide behind screens and meet new people without leaving their homes. Hip-Hop clubs not only brought people together; they also opened doors for talented artists who could rap and perform. Thus, people who did not have a widely known name or large following were able to get a shot (an opportunity) at clubs as well as make connections. There were a lot of big-name artists that performed at these clubs back in the day. Established artists saw up-and-coming people perform and created opportunities for them. There were several different Hip-Hop clubs around New York City that patrons could go to. These included the Rooftop, which was known to be a lot of fun, and the Latin Quarter. The Latin Quarter club was known to be more family oriented. Other well-known clubs in New York at the time included the Fever, Union Square, the Underground, the Zodiac, and Roseland. Each of these clubs had a different vibe. Latin Quarter was more family oriented and usually many of the people there knew one another. For this reason, it was difficult for new, unknown artists to perform at the Latin Quarter. Clubs played a huge role in Hip-Hop's growth and evolution. They allowed a lot of people to express themselves and their "inner Hip-Hop" spirit. They also opened doors for future artists.

CAROL RAFFETY
VIRGINIA TECH

See also:
South Bronx

Further reading:
Ewoodzie, J. C. *Break Beats in the Bronx: Rediscovering Hip-Hop's Early Years.* Chapel Hill: University of North Carolina Press, 2017.
Robbie. "An Oral History of New York's Early Hip-Hop Clubs." Unkut.com, May 14, 2014. www.unkut.com/2014/05/an-oral-history-of-new-yorks-early-hip-hop-clubs/.

Hip-Hop Fashion

In the 1990s Hip-Hop fashion was central to Hip-Hop's growing popularity. Currently one of the biggest names in Hip-Hop fashion is Supreme, which started as a New York skate brand. Supreme has largely capitalized on the style of 1990s street fashion. The nineties was an important decade in terms of Hip-Hop fashion trends. Bone Thugs-n-Harmony and Boyz II Men both created Hip-Hop–oriented styles that influenced other groups of the decade.

The different styles of fashion in the 1980s included the iconic **Kangol hats**, which became popularly associated with LL Cool J in the late eighties and early nineties, and big, bold Pan-African and Afrocentric patterns were worn by pro-black artists like A Tribe Called Quest, De La Soul, the Jungle Brothers, Queen Latifah, and Brand Nubian–together these artists formed the musical collective the Native Tongues. Fashion wise, the Native Tongues distinguished themselves through their African wax print fabrics and bright colors. During the nineties Timberland boots became a classic staple of New York Hip-Hop style. People still wear this type of boot today. Denim jeans are also fashionable today. Leading the way are high-end labels like Guess, Versace, Moschino, and Calvin Klein. Prominent artists who wore a lot of denim during the nineties include Tupac and Eazy-E of N.W.A. In America some of the biggest trends during the nineties surrounded premium American sportswear brands like Tommy Hilfiger, Nautica, and Ralph Lauren's Polo Sport. Wu-Tang Clan came on the scene in 1993 draped in Polo Sport clothing and ready to take their place in Hip-Hop fashion history. During the nineties, when Hip-Hop was characterized by the East Coast–West Coast rivalry, it was not a surprise that sports team apparel came to be a big part of Hip-Hop fashion. Since the 1980s Hip-Hop fashion had included sportswear displaying teams in the NFL, NBA, and NHL. Snapback hats and Starter jackets have been longtime staples of Hip-Hop fashion. Today the brand Supreme features its star logo on the back of its snapback caps as an ode to nineties street style. The first major black-owned Hip-Hop brand was FUBU, which was started by the entrepreneur Daymond John and his three friends. One of the most ubiquitous fashion trends in 1990s gangsta rap was the paisley prints found on bandanas. There were different colors for different gangs; for example, the Los Angeles–based Bloods and Crips wore red and blue bandanas, respectively. In the late eighties bucket hats were popularized by celebrated rap groups like EPMD. The bucket hat style is still popular to this day. Luxury tracksuits by high-end sportswear companies like Nike, Adidas, and Puma have been featured in Hip-Hop since the eighties. Military apparel grew popular with the rise of the group Public Enemy, whose lead vocalist, Chuck D, spoke of the struggles of life as a black person in America. For members of Public Enemy, military uniforms signified their status as soldiers in America's urban warzones. Tupac, Biggie, and Das EFX also wore this type of clothing, which can still be seen in Hip-Hop fashion today.

Other types of clothing that have made their mark in Hip-Hop include Wu Wear T-shirts and hoodies; Coogi sweaters with distinctive, colorful designs; and puffy jackets, born in the streets, and now available from brands like North Face and Helly Hansen. Since their introduction, Air Jordans have held a high status in Hip-Hop along with luxury shoes like Clarks suede wallabees. All of these clothes were worn between the late 1980s and early 1990s in the Hip-Hop fashion world. A lot of these styles are still being worn by people today. People can see that the style from the eighties and nineties has not really changed throughout the years.

Alex Obouh Fegue
Virginia Tech

See also:
Kangol Hats, *Enter the Wu-Tang (36 Chambers)*, *It Takes a Nation of Millions to Hold Us Back*, *Straight Outta Compton*

Further reading:
Foley, G. "21 Trends & Brands That Defined '90s Hip-Hop Fashion." Highsnobiety, March 6, 2019. https://www.highsnobiety.com/p/90s-hip-hop-fashion/.

Hip-Hop Movies

Hip-Hop movies provide a visual representation of the four main components of Hip-Hop culture: deejaying, breaking (break dancing), emceeing, and graffiti. Although the specifications for what qualifies a film to be "Hip-Hop" have been debated, it is generally agreed upon that Hip-Hop movies showcase and focus on one or more components of the art forms surrounding the culture and include a soundtrack filled with Hip-Hop music. Hip-Hop movies helped to popularize this newly emerging genre of music in the 1980s and spread the culture from its birthplace in the **South Bronx** borough of New York City to the rest of the country, and even internationally as well. The use of Hip-Hop movies as a medium to spread Hip-Hop culture helped to bring this new style of music into the mainstream media and out of its underground beginnings. The rest of this entry will detail some notable Hip-Hop movies that have helped Hip-Hop to become the established musical and cultural genre that it is today.

Wild Style

Wild Style, a film released in 1983, is widely considered to be the very first Hip-Hop movie. The movie focuses on the graffiti aspect of Hip-Hop culture and features many founders of Hip-Hop from the 1980s, including Grandmaster Flash and Fab Five Freddy. Set in the South Bronx (which is now defined as the birthplace of Hip-Hop), the film's soundtrack went on to become one of the most fundamental and popular Hip-Hop records of the 1980s.

Beat Street

Beat Street was a film released the following year, 1984. Also set in the South Bronx at the very beginning of the emergence and establishment of Hip-Hop, the film encompasses all four of the main components of Hip-Hop culture (deejaying, graffiti, emceeing, and break dancing). The movie follows the story of a local Hip-Hop crew trying to make it big and showcase their talents outside of New York City. *Beat Street* is credited not just with helping to spread Hip-Hop throughout the United States but also with bringing Hip-Hop culture across international borders, specifically causing a major spike in Hip-Hop's popularity in Germany following the success of the film.

Breakin'

Also released in 1984, *Breakin'* was one of the first Hip-Hop movies not to be set in the recognized birthplace of Hip-Hop, the South Bronx, but instead was set on the opposite coast in Los Angeles, California. This change of setting was important because it showed that Hip-Hop was not just an art form partial to the East Coast but that it had started to spread throughout the continental United States. The film follows the story of a young jazz dancer in LA who takes up break dancing after an encounter with two street dancers. The film goes on to detail her introduction and consequent immersion into the LA break dancing scene. Another significant fact about this movie is that it surpassed the popular coming-of-age film *Sixteen Candles* and became number one in the box office in its release year, validating the new movie genre of Hip-Hop.

House Party

Perhaps the most popular amongst original Hip-Hop movie fans, *House Party* was released in 1990 and starred prominent Hip-Hop duo of the time Kid 'n Play. The movie follows the story of their epic house party and received critical acclaim upon its release. Complete with all of the important components of Hip-Hop, including deejaying, graffiti, and breaking, *House Party* remains a cult favorite in the Hip-Hop community thirty years later.

CB4

CB4, which premiered in 1994, offers a parody of gangsta rap groups and their rise to fame and overall authenticity. The film follows a fictional gangsta rap group—loosely based off of the popular group N.W.A—that pretend to be newly released felons and fake a gangsta lifestyle in order to establish themselves in the world of Hip-Hop. Starring Chris Rock, this satire pokes fun at certain highly critiqued elements of Hip-Hop culture.

Marit Riley
Virginia Tech

See also:
South Bronx, *Straight Outta Compton*

Hip-Hop Names

A name is one of the most important aspects of branding that an artist has in Hip-Hop. It often serves as their very first introduction to the public, before a single bar is even heard. While the names Trevor Smith Jr., Brad Jordan, and Russell Jones leave unremarkable and ultimately forgettable impressions, the chosen names of Busta Rhymes, Scarface, and Ol' Dirty Bastard evoke strong images and intrigue in finding out more about these artists. Giving nicknames is a long-standing cultural tradition in black communities and has played an instrumental role in establishing Hip-Hop artists from the very beginning.

There are many distinct ways that names are formed in Hip-Hop, six of which will be highlighted here. The first and most obvious way is that some people are given incredibly cool birth names like Kanye West, Vince Staples, and Tierra Whack. The second way is similar to the first, but includes slight variations from birth names like Kendrick Lamar Duckworth, Tupac Shakur, and Aubrey Drake Graham, performing as Kendrick Lamar, 2Pac (also written as Tupac), and Drake. The third way is adapting childhood nicknames, which often come from family. Destin Route was called "Jittery" by his grandmother before landing on the name JID; Calvin Broadus was called "Snoopy" by his family because his big ears reminded them of the cartoon character before he decided on the rap name Snoop Doggy Dogg; Juaquin Malphurs was a huge fan of Fozzie Bear and his distinctive catchphrase before landing on the name Waka Flocka.

The fourth way that names are decided is as a way to show allegiance to a group. A$AP Rocky, A$AP Ferg, A$AP TyY, and A$AP Bari all selected names that were slight plays on their birth names, but by including the A$AP in their name they signified a deep allegiance to a crew. The fifth way that names are chosen are in tribute to other cultural hallmarks. Travi$ Scott takes the "Travi$" from his favorite uncle and the "Scott" from Kid Cudi's birth name. B.o.B turns his name into an acronym as a tribute to OutKast's "Bombs Over Baghdad." Both Freeway and Rick Ross take their names from legendary gangster "Freeway" Ricky Ross. The sixth and final way is simply selecting names that sound cool, like André 3000 or Playboi Carti.

TYLER BLANKINSHIP
STUDENTS OF HIP HOP LEGACY (SOHHL)
VIRGINIA TECH

See also:
Doggystyle, Enter the Wu-Tang (36 Chambers)

I

Illmatic

On April 19, 1994, Nasir "Nasty Nas" Jones released a ten-song debut album which became a watershed moment in Hip-Hop's history and development. His seminal album, *Illmatic*, arrived at a time when the East Coast rap scene was in search of a messiah, someone to catapult to the forefront in order to rival the West Coast rap scene's commercial success, seen with the release of Dr. Dre's **The Chronic**. As the album's first single announced: "It ain't hard to tell, I excel, then prevail." Over the last twenty-five years, the taut ten-track reflection of a young black man growing up in the Queensbridge Houses—the largest projects in America—has remained resonant as well as relevant.

"The Genesis" is an effective introductory track because it takes the listener to the geographic heart of the album—six desperate and disparate blocks of the twenty-six Y-shaped apartment buildings that constitute the Queensbridge Houses. It begins with a collage of sounds: the passing of a subway train, dialogue from the classic 1983 Hip-Hop film *Wild Style*, and another clip from Main Source's 1991 song "Live at the Barbeque," in which an eighteen-year-old Nas made his first debut. The journey to *Illmatic* began with "Live at the Barbeque," in which Nas stole the spotlight. Main Source's Large Professor invited Nas to guest on the song, after which they began work on what would become *Illmatic*. Nas's first recorded solo track, "Half Time," appeared on the soundtrack of the 1992 race-relations film *Zebrahead*. The memorable verses delivered by Nasty Nas gained him notoriety, and moreover, being released two years prior to *Illmatic*, it served as the precursor for the album's critical acclaim. The release of the track spurred a Columbia record deal and notoriety which garnered the appearances of some of New York's finest producers for *Illmatic*'s 1994 release. Nas captures the very feeling of being young and trapped, and utilizes *Illmatic* as a vehicle to escape. The album art is an old childhood photograph of Nas, taken by his father, Olu Dara, a veteran jazz musician.

The childhood innocence of young Nas is overlaid on a hazy reflection of the city fading. As listeners hear Nas make sense of his environment, the gaze of this child becomes the mouthpiece through which *Illmatic* gets experienced. Nas raps with a clear-eyed point of view, speaking for himself but also on behalf of the citizens who have lived in the gaping maw of Queensbridge—most notably, he speaks for his dearly departed friend Ill Will, for whom the album is named. The styles and stories that formed Nas fuse into something capable of withstanding years of changes in popular slang and taste: it is the story of a gifted writer born into squalor, trying to claw his way out of the trap. Not only did it establish Nas as the top rapper in the year of 1994, it raised the stakes for Hip-Hop production, lyricism, content, and overall artistic ambition. A classic album is supposed to alter, impact, or serve as a defining factor of the time period of its release; *Illmatic* did all of these.

KENRICK K. CAMERON JR.
VIRGINIA TECH

See also:
The Chronic

Further reading:
Aku, T. "An Oral History of Nas' Classic Debut Album 'Illmatic.'" XXL *Magazine*, April 16, 2014. https://www.xxlmag.com/news/2014/04/making-of-nas-illmatic/.

Fisher, J. "Read the Original 5-Mic Review of 'Illmatic,' Written by Missinfo as a Source Intern." *The Source*, April 19, 2014. http://thesource.com/2014/04/19/today-in-hip-hop-history-nas-released-illmatic/.

Ryu, S. "Straight from the Dungeons of Rap: An Exploration and Oral History of 'Illmatic.'" *Central Sauce*, December 20, 2018. https://centralsauce.com/illmatic-nas-oral-history.

Schwartz, D. "25 Years Later, Nas's 'Illmatic' Remains One of the Best Rap Albums Ever." *Highsnobiety*, April 17, 2019. https://www.highsnobiety.com/p/nas-illmatic-album/.

It Takes a Nation of Millions to Hold Us Back

It Takes a Nation of Millions to Hold Us Back is an album by the Hip-Hop group Public Enemy that was released in 1988. This was the group's second project, with their first being *Yo! Bum Rush the Show*, which was released one year earlier. The group took a different approach on this album and decided to make it have more of an up-tempo sound, which would in turn lead to it having more success than their debut album. *It Takes a Nation* saw a lot of commercial and critical success, with the album charting on the Billboard 200 for forty-nine weeks and eventually being certified platinum by the Recording Industry Association of America (RIAA). To this day, it is still considered by some to be one of the greatest and most influential Hip-Hop albums ever released.

The reason that it is considered to be so influential is due to the content of the album. Public Enemy used this album as a platform to talk about social issues. The album touched on an array of topics, spanning from copyright issues with **sampling** on the song "Caught, Can We Get a

Witness?" to women watching soap operas on "She Watch Channel Zero?!" Yet the main topics discussed in the album were issues surrounding the radio not wanting to play rap music and the state of race relations in the country. For example, in the song "Louder Than a Bomb," the group's front man, Chuck D, raps about how through his pro-black views he is still making an impact on the world despite the FBI wiretapping his phone and thinking that he is a threat—hence the analogy of being louder than a bomb. One of the more successful songs on the album, "Don't Believe the Hype," touched on the issue of commercial radio stations not wanting to play Hip-Hop artists because of the negative stereotypes about black people. In the song, Chuck D says that "In the daytime radio's scared of me" to show the issue that radio stations had with Hip-Hop music at that time.

Not only did Public Enemy display the ability to rap about politically conscious topics but they also displayed their storytelling ability on the song "Black Steel in the Hour of Chaos." This song details the story of a man, through the perspective of Chuck D, who is in prison for dodging the draft and is now planning his escape from prison. While Chuck D is rapping from the perspective of the prisoner, Flavor Flav acts as his conscience, assuring him that he will be able to break out by saying phrases like "We gon' break you outta here" and "We ain't goin' out like that." This album and the content within it would end up laying a blueprint for artists such as Jay-Z and Kendrick Lamar, who would make names for themselves making music that tackles political and social issues.

CHANDLER JONES
VIRGINIA TECH

See also:
Afrocentric Political Rap, College Radio, Sampling

J

James Brown

Mr. Brown was born in Barnwell, South Carolina, on May 3, 1933, sometime before the South was "dirty" and definitely before American mainland geography recognized places of pride for Hip-Hop ability. However, beginning during the 1980s, a generation of rising Hip-Hop artists began utilizing JB's (James Brown's) signature "one-three" beat as inspiration for music that would eventually become what is presently called Hip-Hop.

James Brown was an establishing father of funk and a standout amongst the most significant American perform-ers ever. Brown was a music symbol and pioneer. He was prominently alluded to as the "Godfather of Soul." Brown had both the message and the music to satisfy this title. He additionally put his "good foot" forward with a funky new stable of musicians that later wound up being referred to as the cornerstone of Hip-Hop's infectious instrumenta-tion. It is no happenstance that Mr. Brown is a standout amongst the most examined artists in Hip-Hop still today (check out the "Get Up, Get into It, Get Involved" sample on Nas's "Where Are They Now" from the album *Hip Hop Is Dead*). His rhythmic developments affected most well-known contemporary music styles, including R & B, soul, funk, disco, rock 'n' roll, and, obviously, rap.

Brown's 1970 masterwork "Funky Drummer" stays a stand-out amongst the most sampled tunes in Hip-Hop. The drums have filled in as the spine for multiple tunes by such prominent artists as Nas, Dr. Dre, and Public Enemy. With regards to Hip-Hop, James Brown is the melodic center on which each rap beat was assembled. Rap producers made an art out of gauging their beats in relation to Soul Brother No. 1 (James Brown). Brown blessed us with the driving beat that became the signature sound of Hip-Hop. He truly was the godfather of Hip-Hop.

Through groundbreaking grooves like "Funky Drummer," "Make It Funky," and "Give It Up or Turn It a Loose," Brown made the future on which Hip-Hop would spring. Brown created an unquestionable family relationship with Hip-Hop. Funk is a procedure, a procedure changing one's view of self in reality. One of the best melodies in the historical backdrop of contemporary black music is James Brown's sixties soul classic "Say It Loud, I'm Black and I'm Proud." At no other time had any prominent performer caught the mind-set of black individuals. The recognized founder of Hip-Hop, DJ Kool Herc, has been cited as saying that if not for James Brown, there would no such thing as Hip-Hop.

MICHELLE BERRY
VIRGINIA TECH

See also:
Illmatic, It Takes a Nation of Millions to Hold Us Back, Sampling, *Straight Outta Compton*

K

Kangol Hats

The British headwear brand Kangol was founded in the 1920s after the First World War by a veteran named Jacques Spreiregen. Named after its products' textile components (knitwear, angora, and wool) and portraying a kangaroo logo, the company became the source of berets for British soldiers in the Second World War. Later in the twentieth century, the hats became a trend amongst figures in multiple facets of England's pop culture, such as Princess Diana, the Beatles, and the English Olympic team of 1948.

When the Hip-Hop age emerged in the 1980s, the popularity of Kangol hats expanded and migrated to the United States. By making its way into Hip-Hop culture, the Kangol brand enhanced the era's fashion and became an important accessory of rappers' styles. Hip-Hop artists such as MC Shan, Missy Elliott, and Notorious B.I.G. have all been photographed wearing Kangol headwear. Rapper LL Cool J became famous for wearing a red furry bucket hat with the kangaroo logo in his 1987 music video for the single "I'm Bad." In addition, the hats made their way into film, as they were sported by actors Samuel L. Jackson and Wesley Snipes. Eminem made the Kangol ripstop army hat an aspect of his image when he debuted his music video for the song "Beautiful" in 2009. Kangol hats come in a variety of colors and forms, with the top sellers being the army cap, the 504, and the bucket hat. Based on its reputation spanning over multiple decades in the twentieth and twenty-first centuries, the Kangol brand will continue to have an influence on the style and aesthetics of Hip-Hop artists for years to come.

Isabella J. M. Land
Virginia Tech Fashion Merchandising and Design

See also:
Hip-Hop Fashion

Further reading:
Sanchez, DJ. "Kangol: Over 80 Years of Style, 30 Years of Hip-Hop Influence. *The Source*, April 30, 2018. http://thesource.com/2018/04/30/kangol-over-80-years-of-style/.

L

"La Di Da Di"

"La Di Da Di" is a song created and performed by Doug E. Fresh, also known as the Human Beatbox, and MC Ricky D (presently known as Slick Rick). This song is essential to Hip-Hop's history largely due to Doug E. Fresh's monumental ability to beatbox. This ability surpassed anything that had ever been seen or heard before in the world of Hip-Hop. Slick Rick also has traces of a British accent that struck many people's interest. In "La Di Da Di" these two monumental artists take on different roles. Doug E. Fresh provides **beatboxing** instrumentals (making percussive sounds with one's mouth), while MC Ricky D performs the vocals. Slick Rick also showcased an influential storytelling talent that has since been carried throughout Hip-Hop culture. This song was originally released in 1985 as the B side to the single "The Show." Since its release, the song has been celebrated and is now recognized as a classic from the early Hip-Hop era. It has been both sampled and referenced in a multitude of other songs, including other genres besides Hip-Hop. The song reached number three of Billboard's Hot Black Singles chart and was a top-five hit in England, achieving multiplatinum status worldwide. The song carried so much popularity, it was even released in Spain, Italy, France, and New Zealand. This success led to other opportunities for the duo.

There was also an original vinyl and cassette version released, in which the disco group A Taste of Honey sings a section of the song inspired by the 1960s Japanese hit

"Sukiyaki." However, due to a lack of copyright clearance, many released versions of the song would not include this section. There have also been various artists that created covers of "La Di Da Di." The well-known rapper Snoop Dogg named his cover "Lodi Dodi," the electro-punk band Mindless Self Indulgence covered the song with some changed lyrics, and Chuck Brown and Korn performed their covers live.

KAELA KINDER
VIRGINIA TECH

See also:
Beatboxing, *Doggystyle*, Sampling

M

"The Message"

"The Message" is an extremely iconic song recorded by Grandmaster Flash and the Furious Five. The song originated in Ed Fletcher's (a former songwriter for **Sugar Hill Records**) mother's basement as he played piano and set out to write a song about urban life. It was first released as a single by Sugar Hill Records on July 1, 1982, then released later on the Grandmaster Flash and the Furious Five album titled *The Message*. "The Message" was an influential song in Hip-Hop due to its focus on societal issues. Unlike most Hip-Hop tracks of the era, which included themes of self-infatuation, boasting, and party life, Grandmaster Flash and the Furious Five decided to spread awareness of the culture and environment in which they lived and observed. For example, the song's chorus includes urban descriptions such as, "It's like a jungle sometimes /

It makes me wonder how I keep from going under." This refrain allows outsiders to vividly imagine the struggles that many people of color experienced in urban life. When asked about the song, Flash said, "The subject matter wasn't happy. It wasn't no party shit. It wasn't even some real street shit."

"The Message" was the first hit song of its time to focus on urban social commentary. It took American popular culture by storm and still makes a social impact today. The track sparked a new theme throughout the genre of Hip-Hop and led others to release music about the struggles of inner-city life. Since its release in 1982, the song has continued to gain popularity through video games such as *Grand Theft Auto* and was even performed at the Fifty-Fourth Annual Grammy Awards in 2011. What started as a simple songwriting session turned into one of the most iconic and influential Hip-Hop songs ever to be released.

STEPHEN WILDER
VIRGINIA TECH

See also:
Afrocentric Political Rap, Sugar Hill Records

Further reading:
"The Message by Grandmaster Flash and the Furious Five." Songfacts, n.d.,
        retrieved May 6, 2019. https://www.songfacts.com/facts/grand-
        master-flash-the-furious-five/the-message.

Misogyny in Rap

The portrayal of women in rap music is rarely challenged. Most listeners purchase albums and ignore the lyrics saturated in male chauvinism. Many rappers demean women in their music, perpetuating hegemonic masculinity. Though there are negative representations of women in all genres of music, rap music most heavily depends on these representations, as it is a fundamental aspect of the culture it has amounted to.

The objectification of women in rap music regularly goes undisputed by people in the music industry. When this objectification is brought into question, those in opposition are typically black women and recognized feminists in the Hip-Hop community. So the question becomes, Why do rappers get a pass for disparaging women? Some argue it is part of Hip-Hop culture, while others contend it is a component Hip-Hop could do without.

Many industries rely heavily on patriarchal structures, and Hip-Hop is no exception. From the rhetoric used to describe women in songs to how women are portrayed in music videos, it seems as though disrespecting women is every rapper's default. The reasoning behind this is unclear. Toxic masculinity, an aggregation of cultural lessons that stem from a perceived representation of manhood characterized by dominance and egocentrism, is a common explanation for the continuation of lyrics that shame women. Toxic masculinity is socially destructive because it creates an unrealistic set of norms that men are expected to adhere to. Said norms reinforce an attitude that smears women. How women are portrayed in Hip-Hop exemplifies this.

Another possible explanation for this common practice in rap songs is the idea that "sex sells." Based on this logic, sexually appealing products, especially those with women appearing at the forefront, are more attractive to the market. With this in mind, it must be considered how women in the Hip-Hop music industry like Nicki Minaj and Cardi B are condemned for presenting themselves promiscuously. At the same time, rappers like Ludacris and 50 Cent are revered as men with power and influence when they appear in videos surrounded by half-clothed women. This double standard is apparent in a multitude of institutions, cultures, and practices—not just in Hip-Hop alone. So, the next question is: Does sexism sell? If society is to dismantle the structures that bolster the ego of men at the expense of women, it must deliberate further.

To further examine how masculinity factors into the socialization of black men, one must recognize how society continues to shape the perception of black men. In a whitewashed world, black men are often described as being aggressive and unlawful. Society's impression of black men is largely influenced by a white supremacist ideology that elevates the white man above the black man, and men above women. The idea that rappers must degrade women to conform to the industry is a product of this belief. Interestingly enough, for one to orient themselves against this image would almost be "anti-Hip-Hop" to some. Nevertheless, illuminating these backward traditions is the first step towards sifting out music that belittles women.

This matter is beyond misogyny in rap music. The world views women as sexual beings meant to cater to the needs of men. For many, it goes against the notion of womanhood to stand outside of these principles. From the wage gap between genders to the representation of women in the media, society is laced with sexist undertones. The key to dismembering sexist systems and beliefs is for men to join the fight for women's empowerment. By accepting responsibility and holding one another accountable for actions that maintain male chauvinism, men could be the solution to the headache they created.

DA'ANI JETTON
VIRGINIA TECH

R

"Rapper's Delight"

"Rapper's Delight," released in 1979 by the Sugarhill Gang, is credited with being the first song to introduce Hip-Hop to a wide audience (that is, white and suburban society). At the time, rap music was viewed as inferior, a temporary trend not to be taken seriously by radio stations or traditionally commercialized media. "Rapper's Delight," the original version, is fourteen minutes and thirty-five seconds long, making it one of the longest running songs to be played on the radio. During this time, the average radio audience's attention span was a maximum of three and a half minutes, inferring that "Rapper's Delight" was the first instance of massive love, acceptance, and desire for longer, story-like tracks. Additionally, the Sugarhill Gang hit would be played by radio hosts on their own as well as when requested by listeners, resulting in rap music being heard for thirty minutes, forty-five minutes, even an hour straight, which was positive exposure for the soon-to-be genre of music. "Rapper's Delight" went on to sell over eight million copies—it is purported to have sold fifty thousand copies a day at one point—and was labeled one of the top five hundred songs according to *Rolling Stone* magazine.

The Sugarhill Gang was discovered and produced by **Sugar Hill Records** co-owner Sylvia Robinson. The way in which she recruited the members of the group is up for speculation, but it is said that she heard them rapping at a party and instantly wanted them on a track for her record label. Once in the recording studio, the house band (band supplied by the record label) began to sample (borrow sections from other songs) from the group Chic's hit song "Good Times," using the bass line from the beginning of the song. The rappers would freestyle over the beat, creating what society now knows as the song "Rapper's Delight." However, it has been said that one of the rappers, Wonder Mike, stole his lyrics from well-known deejay and rapper Grandmaster Caz after Caz allowed Mike to borrow his lyric book for inspiration. Some commentators on Hip-Hop culture believe that the Sugarhill Gang and "Rapper's Delight" is a rags-to-riches story, with the average up-and-coming rapper being discovered by chance; however, others perceive the story as perpetuating the idea of benefitting and succeeding from the talents and creations of others.

Despite the somewhat controversial origin story of "Rapper's Delight," its influence helped develop rap music and Hip-Hop culture into the art form it is today. It sustains a feeling of nostalgia and reminds the listener of the fun and clever freestyles as well as the rhythmic and smooth sounds that live at the root of Hip-Hop.

ANASTASIA FREDERICK
VIRGINIA TECH

See also:
Crossover Rap Hits, Cyphers, Sampling

Rick Rubin

Rick Rubin, born Frederick Jay Rubin, co-founded one of the most important record labels in Hip-Hop history. Rubin was born in 1963 in Long Island, New York, with a strong interest in the rising punk scene in New York. Eventually, he became interested in Hip-Hop and in 1984, out of his New York University dorm room, started **Def Jam Recordings**. Under the new label, Rubin and DJ Jazzy Jay produced T La Rock's club hit, "It's Yours." Not long after the song was released, Rubin was introduced to Russell Simmons, who had already produced Kurtis Blow's "Christmas Rappin'" and was managing his younger brother's Hip-Hop group, Run-DMC. After meeting at a nightclub, Rubin brought Simmons on as an equal partner in Def Jam. With Rubin's ear for talent and Simmons's business skills and contacts, the two were a powerful duo.

In 1984 they released the hit single that launched LL Cool J's career, "I Need a Beat." They went on to launch the careers of other artists and groups, such as the Beastie Boys and Public Enemy. One of their most impressive feats was blending rock and Hip-Hop with the Run-DMC and Aerosmith collaboration, "Walk This Way." Many people credit this song with revitalizing Aerosmith's career. The label also oversaw a deal between Adidas and Run-DMC that forecasted Hip-Hop's influence on fashion and pop culture. Overall, Def Jam is recognized as being a major influence in Hip-Hop's transition from an underground or alternative genre to the mainstream.

In 1985 Def Jam Recordings struck a distribution deal with Columbia Records, and following some disputes related to company structure, Rubin left in 1988 and started his own label, Def American Recordings, which he later renamed to just American Recordings. Under his new label, Rubin signed a vast array of different artists, including some heavy metal bands, such as Slayer and the Four Horsemen, and gangsta rap group the Geto Boys. Rubin continued to work with artists still affiliated with Def Jam, such as LL Cool J, Public Enemy, and Run-DMC. American Recordings also had their own rap hits, such as "Baby Got Back" by Sir Mix-A-Lot.

Rubin continued to work with several artists on other labels, such as Jay-Z, the Red Hot Chili Peppers, Tom Petty, AC/DC, Metallica, Shakira, Lil Jon, Kanye West, and Eminem. He's also had a lot of cameo appearances in the music videos of artists he's worked with, such as Eminem's "Berzerk" and Jay-Z's "99 Problems"—Rubin produced both songs. In 2007 Rubin was named co-chairman of Columbia Records and in the same year won the Grammy Award for Producer of the Year. In 2012 he left Columbia to revitalize American Recordings. Rubin continues to work with several artists ranging from country to Hip-Hop and has maintained a high status and respect within the music community for his contributions. Without Rick Rubin, Hip-Hop would not have the popular mainstream status that it has today.

KAYLA MOORE
VIRGINIA TECH

See also:
Christmas Rap, Crossover Rap Hits, Def Jam Records, Hip-Hop Fashion, It Takes a Nation of Millions to Hold Us Back

Further reading:
Ankeny, Jason. "Rick Rubin." All Music, n.d., retrieved May 3, 2019. https://www.allmusic.com/artist/rick-rubin-mn0000356250/credits.

Hirschberg, Lynn. "The Music Man." *The New York Times Magazine*, September 2, 2007. https://www.nytimes.com/2007/09/02/magazine/02rubin.t.html?mtrref=www.google.com.

McDonald, Heather. "Def Jam Records Music Label: The Story Behind the Legendary Def Jam Recordings Music Label." The Balance Careers, March 25, 2019. https://www.thebalancecareers.com/def-jam-records-music-label-profile-2460618.

Roland TR-808 Drum Machine

The creation of the Roland TR-808 drum machine, also known as the "808," was fundamental in revolutionizing Hip-Hop into the music that millions of people know and love today. First introduced in 1980 by Ikutaro Kakehashi, the 808 was constructed in order to allow musicians to program their beats instead of using preset rhythms. Before the 808, producers and musicians would have to find record samples and loop them together by hand in order to create a beat that they wanted. This innovation was monumental in the music world, as there were no programmable drum machines that were as affordable as the 808 at the time. Another aspect that allowed the 808 to stand out was the fact it did not use samples (pre-recorded sounds) to generate its sounds. Instead, the 808 relied on analog synthesis, which electronically creates sounds that were distinct and different from anything ever heard before, as it gave music a futuristic sound. The key to generating these distinct noises was a faulty transistor that Kakehashi deliberately installed in each 808 machine. In 1983 the production of the Roland TR-808 was discontinued because of ongoing critiques about its unrealistic sounds. It was eventually deemed as a flop, selling less than twelve thousand units in its three-year span.

Nearly forty years since its initial release date, the 808 drum machine is as important as ever in the music industry. After its flop on the commercial market, the 808 became a sought-after commodity because no other drum machine in the industry was able to generate the same kinds of unique sounds. The 808 could produce a multitude of percussive sounds, such as snares, toms, congas, rimshots, claves, handclaps, maracas, cowbells, cymbals, and open and closed hi-hats. However, the feature that really led to the 808 becoming a staple in the music industry was its booming bass drum. The 808 is now credited for more hit records than any other drum machine. This success can be attributed to its frequent use with big name Hip-Hop artists, starting with Afrika Bambaataa and his hit song "Planet Rock." Since then, many household names in the Hip-Hop industry have consistently utilized the Roland TR-808 drum machine. For example, Kanye West dedicated a whole album to the drum machine with the release of 808s & Heartbreak, in which every beat on the album was created with an 808 drum machine. In addition to Kanye West, other major artists and producers—such as 808 Mafia, Metro Boomin, Sonny Digital, Zaytoven, Migos, Future, 2 Chainz, and countless others—have produced tracks with the 808 as the key component to their music. Many times, the 808's influence can even be heard in the lyrics of songs, as musicians often give shout-outs to this iconic piece of technology.

Without the creation of the Roland TR-808 drum machine, Hip-Hop would be fundamentally different from how it is today. The 808 provides artists with the chance to incorporate futuristic and unique sounds into their music which they could not find anywhere else. In addition, the 808's electronic generation of sounds ensures that Hip-Hop will never become stale, as new beats and melodies can be created every day. As long as artists and producers continue to utilize the 808 drum machine in their music, the creative potential is endless.

BRETT LEMBKE
VIRGINIA TECH

See also:
Sampling, Universal Zulu Nation

Further reading:
Hasnain, Z. "How the Roland TR-808 Revolutionized Music." The Verge, April 3, 2017. https://www.theverge.com/2017/4/3/15162488/roland-tr-808-music-drum-machine-revolutionized-music.

S

Sampling

Music sampling started in the 1980s, when Hip-Hop first started to gain some attention in the US. People began to experiment with songs and started to try and create new, unique sounds. "Music sampling is the process of lifting a section, such as a drum beat, from a song and including it in a new song" (McGrath).

Deejays in the late seventies and early eighties would use sampling as a way to play the best sections of a song over and over because the people loved the way it sounded and loved dancing to it. DJ Grandmaster Flash helped master the techniques of sampling and began doing different things like changing the speeds of the turntables and also turning them manually. The first sampler was called the Mellotron. "The evolution of hip hop and rap in the 1980 and '90s relied heavily on sampling, often taking samples from" funk music of the seventies and "looping them so they repeat over and over" (McGrath). This all happened naturally. For instance, one day a deejay would simply create a new song and beat by using a recycled song. One of the main goals of sampling was to find snippets of songs with good grooves and loop them as rhythms that were easy to dance to.

Before samplers, Hip-Hop deejays relied on turntables to create these new sounds. In the early eighties, people had just started working with samplers. As time went on samplers became more prominent, and more and more groups started using samplers to create their music. This made their job a little bit easier, but the subsequent enforcement of copyright laws made things tricky.

"As sampling grew in popularity, the copyright laws soon caught up, making it increasingly difficult and expensive to sample music" (McGrath). Initially, Hip-Hop producers did not ask for permission to use someone else's song to make their own beat. As people began to profit off of other artists' work, attention to copyright regulations increased. People who were sampling music had no bad intentions; they simply wanted to create new music using earlier funky beats. Sometimes the original artist who created the song did not pursue legal action when someone else sampled their song. In many cases the company that the artist was contracted with went after the person who sampled the music. Today an artist has to buy the rights to the song or pay the record company that owns the rights a percentage of the profits the artist makes from the new song. Some people could consider sampling stealing someone else's hard work, but others appreciate that the new song has completely original lyrics and a different style to it.

Music sampling has paved a path for all genres of music to create and explore new sounds. Hip-Hop was the first genre to explore these new ways of creating musical sounds and to push the development of how music was made and listened to.

Public Enemy was one of the most popular bands that religiously used sampling to create their music. They wanted to create a distinct musical sound that they could rap over to create something that hadn't been done before.

Sampling has done so much for the Hip-Hop music industry. Sampling allows people to explore their creative side while doing something they love. Most producers are making music for their own enjoyment but also for other people's enjoyment. Hip-Hop sampling in the late 1980s paved the way for future music producers. Although the legal terms of sampling have changed since then, sampling is now a common practice in the music industry. Sampling is good for the music industry because it allows people to explore all genres of music, to make new music out of old music, and to make something musical that they like.

Jack Goonan
Virginia Tech

See also:
Doggystyle, *It Takes a Nation of Millions to Hold Us Back*, James Brown, "La Di Da Di"

Further reading:
McGrath, J. "How Music Sampling Works." HowStuffWorks, June 27, 2011. https://entertainment.howstuffworks.com/music-sampling4.htm.

Scratching

Scratching is one of the most important musical techniques in Hip-Hop. It has been influential in creating original songs and the classic sounds that have been popular in Hip-Hop for years. It is a form or technique that deejays use when they are moving a vinyl record back and forth. This action usually creates a percussive and rhythmic sound that is incorporated into many popular songs. Another word for scratching is *scrubbing*. The vocabulary varies depending on each person's preference. To make the transitions between songs smoother and also undetectable, a crossfader is often used to fade the songs in and out between two vinyl records at the same time. A lot of the time the sounds that are used in scratching include drum beats, horn stabs, spoken word samples, and sometimes vocals or lyrics from sampled songs. Any sound or song that has been recorded to vinyl is up for grabs and is fair game for sampling and scratching. Sometimes materials from songs, television, and samples that are not in vinyl format can be scratched by using a turntable-like surface to scratch sounds that have been burned to a CD-R.

Thanks to the crossover success of pop and Hip-Hop tracks, since 2010 scratching has experienced a resurgence in popularity. The first ever song that was created solely by turntables was "The Adventures of Grandmaster Flash on the Wheels of Steel," created by Grandmaster Flash. The deejay subculture has also developed an underground scratching style that is considered sophisticated and referred to as turntablism. Although scratching is mostly known because of famous Hip-Hop songs, during the 1990s it was used commonly in some rap-rock, rap-metal, and in nu-metal songs. Scratching has been used in so many different genres and subgenres. These genres include rock, jazz, pop, heavy metal, and even some classical music.

Scratching has also been a way to determine the level of skill that a deejay has. There are competitions that deejays from all over the world come to participate in. These competitions are opportunities for deejays to compete against the best of the best. At these competitions, the deejays are only permitted to use equipment that is scratch-oriented. Such competitions are highly anticipated by Hip-Hop deejays everywhere. The deejay with the best scratching, energy, and crowd satisfaction wins.

KENDYL BROOKS
VIRGINIA TECH WOMEN'S BASKETBALL

See also:
Crossover Rap Hits, Sampling

"Self Destruction"

"Self Destruction" is a Hip-Hop single that was released in 1988 primarily as the face of the Stop the Violence Movement. Violence within the Hip-Hop and black communities became increasingly prevalent alongside the rise of unemployment, underfunded schools, and urban decay that disproportionately affected black urban neighborhoods after the Civil Rights movement. Following the murders of Boogie Down Productions founding member Scott La Rock and a young fan that died at a Boogie Down Productions and Public Enemy concert in 1987, KRS-One of Boogie Down Productions created the Stop the Violence Movement to use Hip-Hop as a platform to discuss violence and self-destruction within the black community.

"Self Destruction" is crucial to the history of Hip-Hop in that its creation disregarded economic rewards. Instead, it focused on the essence of an art form that was initially formed to enhance social solidarity in the midst of urban decay. The song was produced by KRS-One, D-Nice, and Hank Shocklee (a producer for Public Enemy) and featured several East Coast rappers, including KRS-One, Doug E. Fresh, Public Enemy, Kool Moe Dee, D-Nice, Stetsasonic, Ms. Melodie, MC Lyte, Just-Ice, and Heavy D. Contributors to the song were committed to the message of antiviolence, as is evident through lyrics such as "I never ever ran from the Ku Klux Klan / And I shouldn't have to run from a black man" and "It's time to stand together in a unity / 'Cause if not then we're soon to be / Self-destroyed, unemployed." Many of the artists contributed to the song in order to be positive role models for black teens surrounded by violence.

The song debuted as the number one song on the first week of Billboard's Hot Rap Songs existence and remained there for ten consecutive weeks. The proceeds from the song went to the National Urban League, which is an advocacy group that was created to alleviate systemic poverty and the poor conditions present in black urban communities. "Self Destruction" was more than a musical commodity. It was the face of a movement dedicated to addressing the omnipresent violence within the Hip-Hop community and larger American culture and to improving the conditions and opportunities for black urban youth.

HAYLIE DECATUR
VIRGINIA TECH SOCIOLOGY

See also:
Afrocentric Political Rap, It Takes a Nation of Millions to Hold Us Back

Further viewing:
McDaniels, R., dir. Overcoming Self-Destruction / The Making of the Self-Destruction Video. United States: BMG Music, 1990. Videocassette (VHS), 60 min.

South Bronx

Many people call the South Bronx the birthplace of Hip-Hop culture. The term South Bronx also became synonymous with urban decay. The white flight (a large-scale migration of whites from racially diverse urban areas to racially homogenous suburban areas) throughout the 1950s and 1960s contributed to the high concentration of poverty in the South Bronx. The racial diversity, combined with other factors, helped create the foundations for Hip-Hop culture.

In the 1970s the popular phrase "The Bronx is burning" described some of the worst instances of urban decay, when landlords began burning down their buildings in an attempt to receive compensation through insurance claims. During the period when the Bronx became plagued with arsons, there were about two to three fires every day for a decade. Another blow to the city was the building of a highway through the heart of the Bronx, which eased the commute for recently relocated white suburbanites. This highway is called the Cross Bronx Expressway.

Along with urban blight, gang activity in the area reached its peak in the early 1970s. By 1972 people grew tired of the loss of life and the gangs came together to sign a peace treaty. The peace treaty deescalated the violence and loosened restrictions on territories, which led to a more creative atmosphere in which Hip-Hop culture could develop. The gangs began to dissipate, but the attitudes and personalities remained. Because of this, certain aspects of the gang culture transferred over to Hip-Hop culture, such as group loyalty and fashion sense.

DJ Kool Herc (Clive Campbell) laid the foundations for Hip-Hop on August 11, 1973, at a South Bronx birthday party where he introduced the technique of breakbeats (the **sampling** of select parts of songs) and began emceeing (rapping) alongside the music. The people who danced to these breakbeats became known as B-boys or break-dancers. Several other deejays built off of this momentum and invented their own techniques that became widely used in Hip-Hop culture. For example, Grand Wizard Theodore (Theodore Livingston) incorporated breakbeats into his music and invented **scratching** (moving a vinyl record back and forth on a turntable in order to create percussive and rhythmic sounds). DJ Afrika Bambaataa became famous for deejaying in the breakbeat style introduced by Kool Herc and for forming a nonviolent Hip-Hop group called the **Universal Zulu Nation** in the Bronx. In addition, Grandmaster Flash invented cutting (the rhythmic repetition of certain portions of a record).

All of these elements of Hip-Hop, invented in the South Bronx, combined to create the culture that exists today. These innovations, in combination with the distinct social conditions, contributed to the South Bronx being titled as the birthplace of Hip-Hop. People recognized the healing power of Hip-Hop culture and used it as an outlet to counter the violence and poverty they were experiencing. Those who contributed to and immersed themselves in the culture found Hip-Hop culture to be healing, as it provided an alternative to the gang activity and condensed poverty. As people began to take notice of the Hip-Hop culture emerging in the South Bronx, it became more popularized, eventually spreading throughout the country and the world.

LEAH GRAVES
VIRGINIA TECH

See also:
Hip-Hop Movies, Sampling, Scratching, Universal Zulu Nation

Spray Paint

Also known as aerosol paint, spray paint is a staple of the Hip-Hop scene. The paint contained within a metal can is propelled out in an aerosol spray when the nozzle is pushed down. Inside the can is a small metal or plastic sphere known as a pea, which facilitates mixing. Spray paint creates a quick, even coat when it is applied. Although spray paint has plenty of commercial and industrial uses, its low price, high availability, portability, and speed of use make it popular for the creation of graffiti, one of Hip-Hop's four main expressive practices.

As the 1970s dragged on, graffiti art became more varied, intricate, and popular. Now, graffiti is recognized as its own unique art form. This evolution has created a market for spray paints specifically designed for graffiti artists. Cans may come equipped with special nozzles, different pressures, unique colors, and multiple peas so that the artists can successfully use varied techniques to create their vision. The medium through which art is created is meaningful, and for this reason spray paint is relevant. Whether cheap spray paint from the hardware store is used to illegally tag territory for a gang in an impoverished neighborhood, or high-quality spray paint is employed to create a piece of graffiti art for a museum, the medium—the spray paint itself—is significant. The iconic dinging of the pea in a shaken spray paint can is easily recognizable in media. This noise is sometimes incorporated into Hip-Hop music, such as in the introduction to Aceyalone's "Mic Check" music video (featuring the song "Calistylics" by CVE).

Spray paint and its use in graffiti is a contentious topic. Tagging is often done illegally and constitutes vandalism. Cities have a difficult time determining what is art and what is crime. Spray paint is central to this unique art form and even Hip-Hop more generally. Spray paint is the medium through which territory is claimed, messages are sent, property is destroyed, and art is created.

JONATHAN TURNER
VIRGINIA TECH

Straight Outta Compton

The album *Straight Outta Compton* was made and produced by the members of N.W.A (Niggaz Wit Attitude)
and released in 1988. The album told personal stories of
the members as they put Hip-Hop in another light. N.W.A
produced a genuine album to explain to listeners the
things occurring within their community, but with a twist.
This group popularized gangsta rapping, which highlights
the gang way of life. This included lots of profanity, which
N.W.A also helped normalize, and descriptions of activities
many people would deem illegal (including crime and violence). *Straight Outta Compton* played a huge role within
Hip-Hop, and N.W.A's influence can still be heard today.
Straight Outta Compton helped many African American
communities realize that they all endure the same struggles, especially when concerning the police. This album
paved the way for the freedom of speech and expression
of anger and distrust of authority within Hip-Hop, which
allowed for other artists to do the same.

The artists featured on *Straight Outta Compton* include
N.W.A members Eazy-E, Ice Cube (who left the group in
1989), MC Ren, Dr. Dre, Arabian Prince, and DJ Yella, who
all were born and raised around Los Angeles, Califor-
nia. The album also featured a guest appearance by Dr.
Dre protégé and future Snoop Dogg mentor the D.O.C.
Straight Outta Compton consisted of thirteen songs and
ran the length of about an hour. The songs listed on the
album are "Straight Outta Compton," "Fuck tha Police,"
"Gangsta Gangsta," "If It Ain't Ruff," "Parental Discretion Iz
Advised," "8 Ball (Remix)," "Something Like That," "Express
Yourself," "Compton's N the House (Remix)," "I Ain't tha 1,"
"Dopeman (Remix)," "Quiet on tha Set," and "Something
2 Dance 2." One of the most popular songs on the album
is the title track, "Straight Outta Compton." This opening
song told the realities of living in Compton (an inner city of
Los Angeles) as an African American. This song wasted no

time expressing the violence and profanity of the gangsta rap that saturated the rest of the album. Another popular song was "Express Yourself." This song went completely against the group's gangsta rap style, which explains its popularity outside of the African American community. This song highlights the realization of self-expression and the importance of people being themselves in a society that tells them to be something that they are not. Another popular song, if not the most popular, is "Fuck tha Police." "Fuck tha Police" is a very explicit song explaining police brutality within and around black communities. This song is still extremely popular within the African American community and is still relevant for African Americans in the United States. This song allowed for the realization that police violence against black people was not only happening within one community or city but happening throughout the country. The song brought lots of backlash from local police forces as well as from the federal government, since the song completely bashed a group of people (police officers) that are usually upheld as the role models in a community. However, "Fuck tha Police" also exposed the harsh realities of police interactions while being African American. The song had a resurgence in popularity immediately following the 1992 LA uprisings.

Straight Outta Compton helped popularize profanity and violence in Hip-Hop and in certain ways made rap music relatable. *Straight Outta Compton* became the blueprint for the style of Hip-Hop music that is popular today.

Zainab Shittu
Virginia Tech

See also:
Afrocentric Political Rap, *AmeriKKKa's Most Wanted*, *The Chronic*

Further reading:
Jenkins, C. "N.W.A, 'Straight Outta Compton' at 25: Classic Track-by-Track Review." *Billboard*, August 8, 2013. https://www.billboard.com/articles/columns/the-juice/5645274/nwa-straight-outta-compton-at-25-classic-track-by-track-review.

Sugar Hill Records

Sugar Hill Records is a record label founded by Sylvia Robinson and her husband, Joe Robinson. The studio was located in Englewood, New Jersey. This record label recognized a market in mainstream music that brought Hip-Hop from the streets to recording studios. The creation of Sugar Hill Records would provide the foundation for Hip-Hop music and artists to spread beyond New York City to the rest of the world.

In the mid-1970s, Sylvia Robinson became interested in the huge Hip-Hop block parties that were happening in New York City. To capitalize upon this music, she decided she wanted to start releasing records. However, she was having trouble gathering interest, as rappers did not believe that the music they made would sell if recorded. She sent her husband to scout for rappers, and eventually they found Wonder Mike, Big Bank Hank, and Master Gee. Together, this group became the Sugarhill Gang that recorded the famous song **"Rapper's Delight."** This song became a top-four smash on the Billboard Hot 100 chart and went number one in several countries around the world. The most successful recording artist on Sugar Hill Records was Grandmaster Flash and the Furious Five. They were able to land eight singles on the R & B charts during their time with the record label. With the Furious Five's single **"The Message,"** Sugar Hill Records was able to cross over to the pop charts for the second time.

The time would eventually come when Sugar Hill Records would experience a major downfall. With other rising rap groups who were changing the sounds of rap, the music Sugar Hill produced became increasingly outdated. Hit with declining commercial fortunes and legal disputes, Sugar Hill Records was forced to close its doors for good in 1986. Then, in 2002, the studio was destroyed by a fire. Many of the label's original recordings, including "Rapper's Delight" and "The Message," would be lost in the fire.

The destruction and downfall of the Sugar Hill record label does not overshadow the impact the company made in the rise of Hip-Hop. The record label paved the way and created the foundation for how Hip-Hop hit mainstream media. It helped Hip-Hop reach others across the world and created interest and taste for the authentic sounds once only heard on the streets of New York. As the first label to produce a rap music video, introduce cassette singles, and televise rap videos when other outlets refused, Sugar Hill Records set up Hip-Hop's successful future.

BRIANA HERNANDEZ
VIRGINIA TECH

See also:
Crossover Rap Hits, "The Message," "Rapper's Delight," Yo! MTV *Raps*

U

Universal Zulu Nation

The Universal Zulu Nation is considered Hip-Hop's first cultural organization and is credited with spreading Hip-Hop internationally. The organization grew out of the Bronx, New York, in 1973. The Zulu Nation began by uniting street organizations such as the Black Spades, Savage Nomads, Seven Immortals, and Savage Skulls. The group was originally named the Organization.

Kevin Donovan, better known as Afrika Bambaataa, and Amad Henderson were essential leaders that developed the Zulu Nation. Afrika Bambaataa is one of the foundational deejays in Hip-Hop along with DJ Kool Herc and Grandmaster Flash. Afrika Bambaataa is known as one of the originators of the breakbeat and electro-funk sound. As his popularity grew, he created the Universal Zulu Nation. The organization's motto is "Peace, love, unity, and having fun." Afrika Bambaataa was inspired by the Civil Rights movement and Civil Rights activists such as Elijah Muhammad and the Black Panthers. Bambaataa's worldviews were completely changed after a trip to Africa, where he visited communities in Nigeria, the Ivory Coast, and Guinea-Bissau. The trip was one of the factors that inspired him to create communities in America that were similar to what he experienced in Africa. The movie *Zulu* was another factor that influenced Bambaataa's perspectives. The movie depicted the solidarity and fierceness that Zulu warriors used to expel the imperial rule that the British were trying to place on the indigenous peoples of Africa. The unity displayed in the movie spoke to Afrika Bambaataa. All of these experiences led him to think of culture as a creative outlet that could be used to move communities towards peaceful ways of expression.

The Zulu Nation views Hip-Hop as a way to break down cultural barriers in order to express the oppression and struggles that are common in all societies. Additionally, the Universal Zulu Nation was created as a music-focused youth organization. As a reformed Black Spade, Afrika Bambaataa understood the destruction and negative influence that came from being involved with gangs. Therefore, the organization's efforts helped provide an alternative to gang involvement by offering music lessons and musical entertainment through community parties. It was not easy to get all the gangs to stop fighting, but through the power of Hip-Hop gangs began their transition from individual groups to a force united under their collective love for the music. Hip-Hop music was able to lower the violence levels and create a calmer environment in and around New York City.

The influence of the Universal Zulu Nation grew as Afrika Bambaataa began to travel not only all around the United States but also internationally. Afrika Bambaataa and the Zulu Nation went on their first world tour in 1982, bringing Hip-Hop to locations that had never heard anything like it before. The organization boasts chapters in twenty different countries and over ten thousand members worldwide. Although it is an Afrocentric organization, people of all races and ethnicities are welcomed to join because the group recognizes that there is oppression everywhere; therefore, Hip-Hop can be used to peacefully spread a message and evoke a voice for those victims suffering from oppression. Current members center themselves around lessons of empowerment by radiating love, seeing themselves as all-powerful, and needing to spread the lessons they have come to live by. To reinforce confidence and pride in themselves and their culture, all members call each other "Kings" and "Queens." The Zulu Nation focuses on what they call "facts of the universe," meaning that all books should be read with an open mind and analyzed for facts, truths, and falsehoods.

Although the Universal Zulu Nation was largely influential during the early Hip-Hop era, it has started to lose relevance within the Hip-Hop community. Fewer and fewer people in today's Hip-Hop community recognize the important role that the Universal Zulu Nation played in spreading the influence of Hip-Hop throughout America and internationally.

JESSICA MUZO
VIRGINIA TECH

See also:
South Bronx

Y

Yo! MTV *Raps*

Yo! MTV *Raps* was the first Hip-Hop music video program produced by MTV that featured a combination of rap videos, interviews, comedy, and live studio performances. The two-hour show ran on the air from August 1988 through August 1995. As Yo! MTV *Raps* entered the nineties, it began to solidify itself as a cultural staple in broadcast television. It gave rap fans located outside of Hip-Hop's major cities, such as New York and Los Angeles, the opportunity to watch and listen to their favorite artists from the comfort of their homes. Regardless of age or race, music lovers were instantly introduced not only to both African American and some Latino sounds but to their styles, traditions, and cultures as well.

The original airing of Yo! MTV *Raps* was hosted by American visual artist, filmmaker, and rapper Fab 5 Freddy. As one of Hip-Hop's pioneers, Fab 5 Freddy provided the show's viewers with the information and context required for understanding this new genre of music and the cultural lifestyle which surrounds it. For the inaugural year of Yo! MTV Raps, new episodes were only aired over the weekend; however, due to the show's high ratings and positive reviews, the network premiered a weekday version of the show titled Yo! MTV Raps Today on March 13, 1989. The weekday version, with hosts Ed Lover and Doctor Dre (not to be confused with N.W.A member Dr. Dre), became a cultural phenomenon, as its name would be referenced through various television shows, such as Doogie Howser, M.D. and Full House.

It was due to this universal acknowledgment that other broadcasting stations began programing their own versions of Hip-Hop culture. BET Network's Rap City premiered in January of 1989 and became Yo! MTV Raps' chief competition up until latter's cancelation. Unfortunately, as gangsta and hardcore rap began to develop, Yo! MTV Raps started to fall in ratings due to showing content that was considered too violent. Eventually, the show came to a conclusion on August 17, 1995, after broadcasting its historic series finale **cypher**. It featured some of Hip-Hop's largest moguls, like Rakim, KRS-One, and Erick Sermon, among others.

From 1996 to 1999 the network chose to "re-create" the once admired program and changed the name to Yo!, dropping the MTV Raps portion of the title. The repackaged version would rotate a cast of different hosts from episode to episode, replacing the three original hosts: Fab 5 Freddy, Ed Lover, and Doctor Dre. By 1998 Yo! had no guest hosts and shortened to an hour-long program, airing at either 1:00 or 2:00 a.m. The show experienced a number of replacements, going from Yo! to *Direct Effect* and eventually to *Sucker Free* in 2006. However, regardless of how the program changed, the original incarnation of the television show still holds dear to OG (original gangster, authentic) rap fans. In addition, the program has expanded through technology, reaching younger generations with applications like YouTube. Yo! MTV *Raps* gave Hip-Hop the visual tools required to spread its sounds and style, allowing rap culture to grow into the mainstream genre it is today.

Nick Payne
Virginia Tech

See also:
Cyphers, Straight Outta Compton

Further reading:
Brown, P. "The Amazing Oral History of 'Yo! MTV Raps.'" Vibe, June 1, 2018. https://www.vibe.com/2018/06/oral-history-of-yo-mtv-raps.

About the Editors

Anthony Kwame Harrison is the Edward S. Diggs Professor of Humanities and associate professor of sociology at Virginia Tech. He is the author of two books—*Hip Hop Underground* (Temple University Press, 2009) and *Ethnography* (Oxford University Press, 2018)—and co-editor of *Race in the Marketplace: Crossing Critical Boundaries* (Palgrave Macmillan, 2019). Kwame currently serves on the editorial boards for the *Journal of Popular Music Studies* and the Bloomsbury Popular Music digital resource (www.bloomsburypopularmusic.com).

Craig Arthur is assistant professor and Head of Foundational Instruction and Community Engagement for Virginia Tech's University Libraries. He started deejaying in 1997 and is a member of the Table Rok Crew. An alumnus of Virginia Tech, he conducted research as an undergraduate with #VTDITC Advisory Board member Dr. A. Kwame Harrison, which ultimately led him to a career in librarianship. As a deejay, he has shared stages with many artists, including Kanye West, Common, Little Brother, the Vinyl Junkies Clique, Mike Jones (who?), and Lil Yachty. To safeguard his honorific "the nicest librarian on two turntables," he eagerly awaits any challenges from fellow librarian deejays.

Made in the USA
Columbia, SC
06 September 2021